NIKOLA TESLA

MASTERMINDS

IZZI HOWELL

First published in Great Britain in 2020 by Wayland, an imprint of Hachette Children's Group, part of Hodder & Stoughton.

All inquiries should be addressed to:
Peterson's Publishing, LLC
4380 S. Syracuse Street, Suite 200
Denver, CO 80237-2624
www.petersonsbooks.com

ISBN: 978-1-4380-8936-2

All words in **bold** appear in the glossary on page 30.

Printed in China

MIX
Paper from responsible sources
FSC® C144853

Picture acknowledgements:
Alamy: IanDagnall Computing 4, David Monette 17, RTRO 20, Science History Images 23, Everett Collection Inc 28; Getty: ullstein bild cover, clu 8t, Alexander Jung 9t, Schenectady Museum; Hall of Electrical History Foundation/Corbis 13, ZU_09 and Nastasic 14, Universal History Archive/Universal Images Group 16, sergey02 18–19b, Bettmann 19t and 26, Stefano Bianchetti/Corbis 21, FPG/Archive Photos 22, ilbusca 25r; Library of Congress: Historic American Buildings Survey 18t; Shutterstock: Igor Smolnikov 5, Ilija Ascic 6, NikolaR 7, givaga 8–9b, Everett Historical 10 and 12, Alted Studio 15, Prachaya Roekdeethaweesab 25l and 30, Paramonov Alexander 25c, e2dan 27t, Sakala 27b, saiko3p 29t, Grzegorz Czapski 29b; Wikimedia: Matejpavel1 24.
All design elements from Shutterstock.

Every effort has been made to clear copyright. Should there be any inadvertent omission, please apply to the publisher for rectification.

The website addresses (URLs) included in this book were valid at the time of going to press. However, it is possible that contents or addresses may have changed since the publication of this book. No responsibility for any such changes can be accepted by either the author or the publisher.

All facts and statistics were correct at the time of press.

CONTENTS

WHO WAS NIKOLA TESLA?

Nikola Tesla was a Serbian-American inventor and **engineer**. He developed the system of electricity that we use in homes and businesses today. This system is known as alternating current (AC) (see page 11).

Nikola's family was Serbian, but he spent most of his adult life in the USA.

Nikola also developed many other inventions, including the induction **motor** (see page 9) and the Tesla coil—a system of transferring electricity without wires (see page 19). Tesla coils were used in radio **transmitters** and in many of Nikola's other experiments.

Electricity can shoot out into the air from a Tesla coil. Today, they are often seen in museums.

CHILDHOOD

Nikola was born on July 10, 1856 in the town of Smiljan, which is in present-day Croatia. He was one of five children. His father, Milutin, was an **Orthodox** priest and his mother, Djuka, ran the household. She liked inventing small machines, such as a mechanical eggbeater, in her free time.

Nikola's childhood home still stands today in Smiljan. It has been turned into a museum with information about his life.

Nikola's intelligence was clear from an early age. His teachers couldn't believe that he was able to do complicated math calculations in his head and wrongly accused him of cheating.

Nikola's father wanted him to become a priest, but Nikola was certain that he wanted to study science and become an engineer.

At the age of 14, Nikola moved to the city of Karlovac to go to high school. In science class, the teachers carried out experiments with electricity that caught Nikola's attention.

GROWING UP

In 1875, Nikola went to college in Graz, Austria, to study engineering. At college, he saw a Gramme **dynamo** for the first time. This machine can generate electricity or work as an electric motor. It fascinated Nikola.

The Gramme dynamo uses magnets to generate direct current (DC) electricity (see page 11).

The Technical
University in
Graz is still
open today and
continues to
welcome many
students.

In 1881, Nikola moved to Budapest, Hungary to work for the Central Telephone Exchange as a chief electrician. While he was in Budapest, he started designing an induction motor. This was a new type of electric motor that was powered by alternating current. Nikola would finish his design years later in New York City (see page 15).

When Nikola was young, Hungary was located in the Austro-Hungarian **Empire**, along with other countries. This empire lasted until the end of World War I (1914-18).

Danube River, Budapest

In the second half of the nineteenth century, many scientists were **researching** new ways to generate electricity and supply it to buildings. One of the most important electricity **pioneers** from this time was Thomas Edison (1847–1931), who was a businessman and inventor.

By the time of his death, Edison had been granted over 1,000 **patents,** including 389 for electric light and power.

At that time, the main sources of artificial light were gaslights, oil lamps, and candles. Thomas's **laboratory** developed the first commercially successful light bulb, followed by a system that supplied electricity to buildings. His system used direct current. Thomas didn't want to work with alternating current because he thought that it was dangerous.

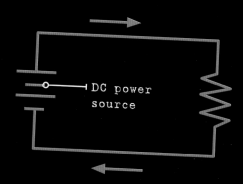

Direct current (DC)

DC power source

In a DC circuit, current only flows in one direction.

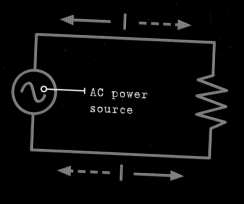

Alternating current (AC)

AC power source

In an AC circuit, current can change direction.

In 1882, Nikola started working for the Continental Edison Company in Paris, France. This was an electrical company founded by Thomas Edison that installed electric lights in homes and businesses.

Nikola traveled to other branches of the company across Europe to help with their designs. He had a great knowledge of physics and was able to quickly fix problems and find solutions.

The lights in Thomas's system were powered by direct current, which was created by huge **generators.**

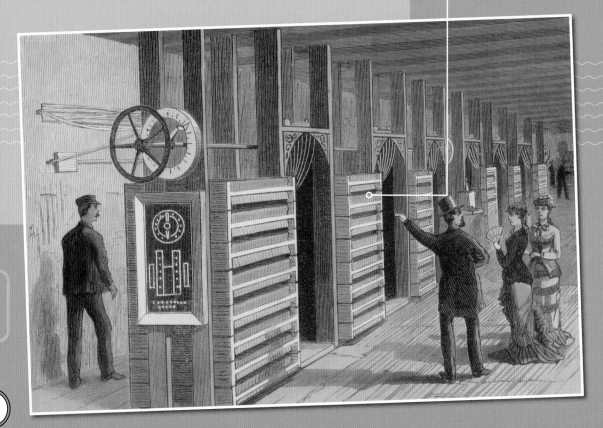

Nikola moved to New York City in 1884. He found a new job in an electrical system equipment factory owned by Thomas Edison. It was a busy and crowded place to work and Nikola didn't have many opportunities to be creative. He quit after only six months.

In the factory, workers made generators and other pieces for Thomas's electrical systems. Nikola's job was to improve the design of the equipment and solve any problems.

After leaving Thomas's company, Nikola worked on his own designs for electric motors, generators, and lamps. He started his own company called Tesla Electric Light and Manufacturing—along with two businessmen—in order to sell his designs.

Then, the two businessmen decided that they only wanted to supply electricity. They took the patents for Nikola's designs and started a new company, leaving him with nothing.

Many other designs for electrical motors, generators, and machinery were being developed at the same time by other inventors.

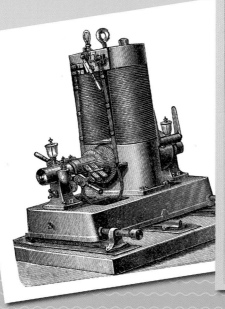

In 1887, Nikola found two **investors** who gave him money to set up his own laboratory. There, Nikola finished his design for the AC induction motor. This was the first motor that worked with alternating current. Nikola also developed a system to bring AC electricity to homes and businesses.

This is a model of Nikola's AC induction motor.

In 1888, an electrical **entrepreneur** called George Westinghouse bought the patent to Nikola's AC electrical system. His business began to install AC systems across the USA. Thomas Edison was very unhappy about this, as it took customers away from his DC system.

Nikola gave lectures on his AC electrical system, explaining how it worked and why it was safe.

George Westinghouse's company supplied electric lighting for the 1893 **World's Fair** in Chicago (seen here). This was an important moment in the War of the Currents, as the many people who attended saw the safe and reliable AC lighting system firsthand.

Thomas started a campaign against alternating current, claiming that it was dangerous because it had a high **voltage**. However, Nikola's system used **transformers** to change the voltage before it went into people's homes, making it safe.

Both men fought hard to make their system the main source of electricity. This was known as the War of the Currents. In the end, alternating current was more popular and it became widely used. Today, direct current is only produced by batteries and solar panels.

NEW PROJECTS

After winning the War of the Currents, Nikola and George worked together on another exciting project. They installed generators at Niagara Falls to produce AC electricity. This electricity was sent to the nearby town of Buffalo, New York to be used by homes and businesses.

This is one of the generators designed by Nikola that was installed in the **hydroelectric** power plant at Niagara Falls.

Niagara Falls is a group of waterfalls on the border between the USA and Canada. Hydroelectric power plants are still used there today to generate electricity.

The success of Nikola's AC system and generators gave him enough money to rent his own laboratory. This meant that he could spend more time working on his own projects and ideas.

During this time, Nikola came up with his final design for the Tesla coil, a steam-powered electricity generator, and a radio-controlled boat. He also experimented with **X-rays**.

Nikola loved studying machines and how they worked.

WIRELESS POWER

Nikola was very interested in the idea of wireless power. He thought that he might be able to send electricity through the air or through Earth itself. He hoped that eventually we would also be able to communicate wirelessly.

Today, Nikola's prediction has come true, and we use many wireless forms of communication, such as mobile phones and the Internet.

This drawing shows Nikola's idea for how wireless power could be sent through Earth to different countries, or even boats at sea.

Nikola wanted to test what would happen when electricity was sent through different types of air. He set up a new laboratory in Colorado at a very **high altitude**. There, he proved that electricity could be sent through Earth. He managed to light 200 lamps wirelessly from a distance of 24.8 miles.

In his experiments with wireless power, Nikola used a very large Tesla coil to generate electricity. This photo shows him sitting close to a Tesla coil to demonstrate that his invention is safe.

After his successful research in Colorado, Nikola wanted to build a large transmitter to send electricity across greater distances. He began building a huge transmitter tower in New York City called Wardenclyffe Tower.

However, Nikola couldn't find investors to help pay for the project. He eventually ran out of money and had to stop his research.

Wardenclyffe Tower was knocked down in 1917.

After this disappointment, Nikola struggled financially. He spent years working on new designs for machines, such as **turbines**, but he was never able to test his ideas because he didn't have enough money.

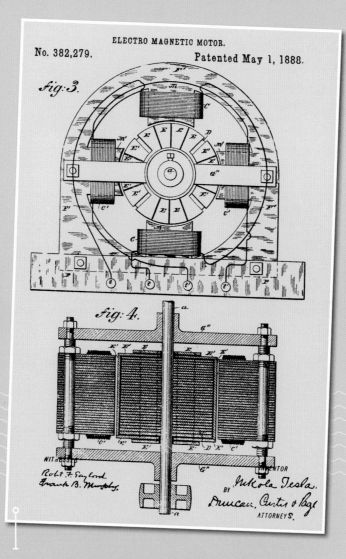

ELECTRO MAGNETIC MOTOR.

No. 382,279. Patented May 1, 1888.

Fig. 3.

Fig. 4.

Over time, Nikola received less money from his patents for previous inventions, such as the electromagnetic motor (shown here).

AWARDS

Throughout his life, Nikola received many awards for his work in different countries, including the USA, Serbia, and France. In 1917, he won the Edison Medal, which is the oldest and the most important award for electrical engineers in the USA.

Nikola was awarded the Collar of the Order of the White Lion by the Czech Republic in 1937. This is an award for non-Czech citizens who have achieved great things.

In 1915, there were rumors that Nikola was going to share a Nobel Prize with Thomas Edison. The Nobel Prize is a very important honor for scientists. However, in the end, neither Nikola nor Thomas was **nominated** for the award.

Some people think that Nikola and Thomas weren't nominated for the award because the two enemies wouldn't have been willing to share the prize.

ALFR· NOBEL

NAT· MDCCC XXXIII OB· MDCCC XCVII

Nikola Tesla

Thomas Edison

LATER LIFE

As he grew older, Nikola lived in many different hotels in New York City. Since he didn't have much money, he always left without paying the hotel bill. He threw a big party for his 75th birthday, and several other birthdays after that. He invited journalists to the parties to tell them about his new ideas for inventions.

This photograph was taken of Nikola at the age of 76 in 1933.

Nikola died on January 7, 1943 at the age of 86. Around 2,000 people attended his funeral in New York City. Later, many of his belongings were sent to Belgrade, Serbia. Today, they are displayed in the Nikola Tesla Museum in Belgrade.

A large Tesla coil at the Nikola Tesla Museum.

Nikola's ashes are held inside this gold sphere, which is on display at the Nikola Tesla Museum.

REMEMBERING TESLA

Today, we remember Nikola for his contribution to science and the major impact that his safe, simple AC electricity supply has had on our society. Many books have been written about his life and inventions.

The 2019 film *The Current War* is the story of the competition between direct and alternating current in the nineteenth century. The actor Nicholas Hoult played Nikola Tesla.

Many objects have been named after Nikola Tesla. Some are his own inventions, such as the Tesla coil. A crater on the Moon has also been named "Tesla" in his honor. One of the most famous uses of Nikola's name today is the company Tesla Inc., which produces electric cars and solar panels.

The airport in Belgrade, Serbia is named after Nikola Tesla.

Some Tesla cars have eye-catching features, such as doors that open upward instead of outward.

GLOSSARY

dynamo: A device that changes movement energy into electrical energy

empire: A group of countries ruled by one person or country

engineer: Someone whose job it is to design new machines or structures

entrepreneur: Someone who starts and develops a new business

generator: A machine that produces electricity

high altitude: At a great height

hydroelectric: Producing electricity from the movement of fast-flowing water

investor: Someone who gives money to a project to make a profit later

laboratory: A room used for scientific work, such as research and experiments

motor: A machine that turns electricity or fuel into movement to make a machine work

nominated: To be suggested for an award or honor

Orthodox: A branch of the Christian Church

patent: The legal right to make and sell an invention for a certain length of time

pioneer: One of the first people to do something

research: Studying something in order to get more information about it

transformer: A device that changes the voltage of an electrical current as it moves from one circuit to another

transmitter: A piece of equipment for broadcasting radio or TV signals

turbine: A machine that produces power when liquids or gases turn a special wheel as they flow through it

voltage: The force of an electric current

World's Fair: A large international exhibition designed to show the achievements of different countries

X-ray: A type of energy ray

TIMELINE

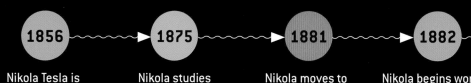

1856
Nikola Tesla is born in Smiljan, in present-day Croatia.

1875
Nikola studies engineering at college in Graz, Austria.

1881
Nikola moves to Budapest, Hungary, to work as the chief electrician for the Central Telephone Exchange.

1882
Nikola begins working for the Continental Edison Company, founded by Thomas Edison, in Paris, France.

BOOKS

Who Was Nikola Tesla?
by Jim Gigliotti
(Penguin Workshop, 2018)

Nikola Tesla and Thomas Edison (Dynamic Duos of Science)
by Robyn Hardyman
(Gareth Stevens Publishing, 2014)

Nikola Tesla for Kids: His Life, Ideas, and Inventions
by Amy M. O'Quinn
(Chicago Review Press, 2019)

WEBSITES

www.pbs.org/newshour/science/5-things-you-didnt-know-about-nikola-tesla
Discover eight fun facts about Nikola Tesla.

www.biography.com/inventor/nikola-tesla
Read a biography of Nikola Tesla.

www.bbc.co.uk/programmes/p00kvnws
Watch a demonstration of a Tesla coil.

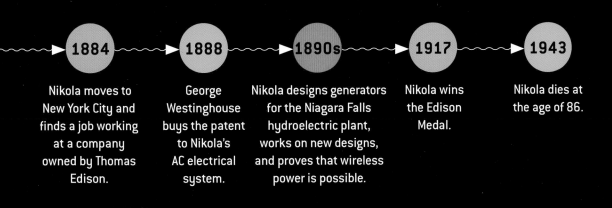

1884
Nikola moves to New York City and finds a job working at a company owned by Thomas Edison.

1888
George Westinghouse buys the patent to Nikola's AC electrical system.

1890s
Nikola designs generators for the Niagara Falls hydroelectric plant, works on new designs, and proves that wireless power is possible.

1917
Nikola wins the Edison Medal.

1943
Nikola dies at the age of 86.

INDEX

More titles in the the **Masterminds** series

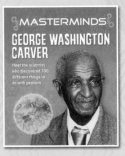

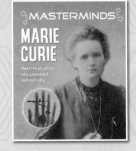

• Who was George
Washington Carver?
• Childhood • Freedom
• Getting an Education
• College Days • The
Tuskegee Institute
• Soil Problems
• New Crops
• Switching Over
• Peanut Products
• Teaching • Later Life
• Remembering Carver

• Who was Marie Curie?
• Childhood • Studies
in France • Meeting
Pierre • Studying Rays
• New Discoveries
• Radioactive Radium
• Working Hard • Family
• Teaching and Learning
• World War I
• Later Years
• Remembering
Marie Curie

• Who is Jane Goodall?
• Childhood • Off to
Africa • Ancestors and
Evolution • Living with
Chimpanzees • New
Discoveries • Back to
School • Family
• Inspiring Others
• Spreading the Word
• The Jane Goodall
Institute • Activism
• Celebrating Jane
Goodall

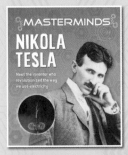

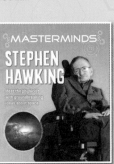

• Who was Katherine
Johnson?
• A Bright Beginning
• Getting Ahead
• Teaching and Family
• A New Job
• Fighting Prejudice
• Into Space
• In Orbit • To the Moon
• Later life • *Hidden
Figures* • Celebrating
Katherine Johnson
• A New Generation

• Who was Nikola Tesla?
• Childhood
• Growing Up
• Electricity and Edison
• Moving to the USA
• Branching Out
• The War of the Currents
• New Projects
• Wireless Power
• Struggles
• Awards
• Later life
• Remembering Tesla

• Who was Stephen
Hawking? • Childhood
• College days
• Family • Space-time
Study • Black Holes
• A New Voice • Sharing
Science • The Future
• Adventures • *The
Theory of Everything*
• Awards • Remembering
Stephen Hawking